The
Man-Made Famine
in Ukraine

The Man-Made Famine in Ukraine

Robert Conquest
Dana Dalrymple
James Mace
Michael Novak

American Enterprise Institute for Public Policy Research
Washington and London

Library of Congress Cataloging in Publication Data
Main entry under title:

The Man-made famine in Ukraine.

  (AEI studies ; 404)
    1. Ukraine—Famines—Congresses.   2. Collective farms
—Ukraine—History—Congresses.   3. Soviet Union—
Economic policy—1928–1932—Congresses.   I. Conquest,
Robert.   II. American Enterprise Institute for Public
Policy Research.   III. Series.
HC337.U5M24 1984   363.8'0947'71   84-2951
ISBN 0-8447-3552-3

ISBN 0–8447–3552–3
1 3 5 7 9 10 8 6 4 2

AEI Studies 404

Printed in the United States of America

Participants

ROBERT CONQUEST, a senior research fellow and curator of the Russian and East European collection at the Hoover Institution, is an adjunct fellow at the Center for Strategic and International Studies at Georgetown University.

DANA DALRYMPLE, a specialist in international agricultural research with the U.S. Department of Agriculture, has written on Soviet agricultural technology for *Agricultural History, Technology and Culture*, and *Soviet Studies*.

JAMES MACE, a postdoctoral fellow at the Harvard Ukrainian Research Institute, is the author of *Communism and the Dilemmas of National Liberation: National Communism in Soviet Ukraine, 1918–1933*.

MICHAEL NOVAK, who holds the George Frederick Jewett Chair for Public Policy Research at the American Enterprise Institute, is the author of *The Spirit of Democratic Capitalism* and *Confession of a Catholic*.

Michael Novak

I am delighted to welcome all of you here on behalf of the American Enterprise Institute for this seminar discussion on the immense famine that took place fifty years ago. We meet in a century of great bloodshed, of many massacres and terrors. Even as we meet, the radio talk shows are dominated by comments on the plight of 269 persons who plunged to their death in a Korean airliner in twelve minutes as they hurtled down from 35,000 feet. In these talk shows, many callers express their disbelief that rational people could contrive the shooting down of a passenger plane. Reasonable people, they say, could not do such a thing; it must have been an accident. It has always—and not only in our age—been difficult to plumb the meaning of reason and the capacity of human beings to do evil. Yet it is impossible to discuss foreign policy as a reasonable way of conducting human affairs without addressing subjects that force such questions upon us. Today we will concern ourselves with one such subject.

I will introduce the speakers now in reverse order. Dr. Dana Dalrymple, our third speaker, is appearing as a private individual, not as a representative of the U.S. government, although he is an agricultural economist with the U.S. Department of Agriculture. Dr. Dalrymple wrote the first comprehensive essay on the great famine of the year 1933 almost twenty years ago.[1] A specialist in international agricultural research, he earned the bachelor of science and master's degrees at Cornell University and took his Ph.D. at Michigan State University, concentrating on agricultural economics with a minor in Soviet studies. Intrigued by how little was known in the West about the great famine of 1933, Dr. Dalrymple undertook research on his own time and on his own initiative and has continued to follow literature on the famine.

We are also privileged to have with us Dr. James Mace, who is currently a postdoctoral fellow at the Harvard Ukrainian Research

---

1. Dana G. Dalrymple, "The Soviet Famine of 1932-34," *Soviet Studies*, January 1964, pp. 250-84; "The Soviet Famine of 1932-34: Some Further References," *Soviet Studies*, April 1965, pp. 471-74.

Institute. He is collaborating on research for a most important book by Dr. Conquest on the Ukrainian famine that will appear next year. Dr. Mace took his baccalaureate at Oklahoma State University and his Ph.D. at the University of Michigan, where he wrote a doctoral dissertation on national communism in Soviet Ukraine in the 1920s. He has studied with the noted Ukrainian author and historian Professor Roman Szporluk. Dr. Mace has written many articles and is currently investigating documents in the Ukrainian language on the famine.

Dr. Robert Conquest, who will be our first speaker, is currently senior research fellow and curator of the Russian and East European collection at the Hoover Institution at Stanford University, a research associate at Harvard University, and an adjunct fellow at the Center for Strategic and International Studies at Georgetown University. Born and educated in Great Britain, Dr. Conquest holds degrees from Oxford University. He is a member of the editorial board of *Continent* and also sits on the advisory board of the Institute for European Defense and Strategic Studies in London. He has served as a United Kingdom delegate to the United Nations and has received the Order of the British Empire. He has written many scholarly books and articles. He is currently completing the book on the Ukrainian famine that I mentioned earlier. In the meantime Dr. Conquest continues to write a column that appears each month in the *Daily Telegraph* and elsewhere.

Robert Conquest

Since time is limited, I will simply review events and our present state of knowledge, because I find that people do tend to muddle the sequence slightly; I did so myself until I started studying the subject.

During the winter of 1929, there occurred the first wave of dekulakization, the arrest in this case of all the worst so-called kulaks—the ones who had been somehow involved in an anti-Soviet regime or army or demonstration or who were accused of having done so at some time. Such people were many in a country that had had a great civil war. Once arrested, they were shot or sent to prison camps. From January to March 1930, there occurred the crash collectivization of virtually all farms and the second dekulakization, the sending off to the north and to Siberia of millions of people who were simply the more affluent peasants. There ensued endless revolts, strikes of the peasantry, the slaughter of the cattle, and the failure of the campaign.

In March 1930, Stalin issued the famous article "Dizzy with Success," ordering the authorities to allow the peasants to leave the collective farms. Most of them did so. During the following eighteen months or two years, pressure was brought to bear less abruptly but just as relentlessly, and they were gradually forced back into the collectives again. When the peasants left, they could not in any case take their implements. By mid-1932, after several other waves of deportation of people alleged to be kulaks—that is to say, influential villagers of any sort—the main parts of the countryside had been almost totally collectivized, in particular in Ukraine, about which we are now talking.

Thus the events of 1933 had nothing to do with dekulakization, which had already taken place. The two episodes are often confused.

In August 1933, however, grain delivery requirements for Ukraine were set far in excess of the region's capacity. This was the key moment.

Perhaps the best short account of the whole fate of the peasantry is one chapter in Vasily Grossman's book *Forever Flowing*, which was published here by Harper and Row. The story is in fictional form. Grossman wrote a great novel that was seized in the early 1970s, and afterward he dashed off this one just before he died. It is not as good as it might be; but the chapter on the peasantry is outstanding, and even the translation is quite good. Grossman writes, "I think there has never been such a decree in all the long history of Russia, not the tsars, nor the Tartars, nor the German occupiers, ever promulgated such a terrible decree. For the decree required that peasants of Ukraine, the Don, and the Kuban be put to death by starvation, put to death along with their little children."

By the beginning of the winter, all the grain, including the seed grain of the farms in Ukraine, had been seized by the government. The peasants lived on the last remaining potatoes, killed their last remaining livestock, they slaughtered cats and dogs, ate nettles and linden leaves. The acorns were all gone by about January, and people began to starve. By March no food at all remained, and they died. The children died first, mostly the younger children, followed by the older people, then usually the men before the women, and finally everyone else. Death did not overtake the entire population, but it occurred on a very large scale and eliminated many whole villages.

The people who died included those who had remained poor despite the fact that land had been divided and given to them twice in two different cycles in twelve years. These so-called "poor peasants" were mostly the village rabble whom the regime had used to extract the grain and who had searched with great rods in every bit of the land and in every house. Their efforts did not do them very much good.

I have given only a very brief outline of events. Now we must consider why they happened. One factor that of course does not apply only to Ukraine was that the Bolsheviks hated the peasantry. In this respect the Bolsheviks were not alone. Very much the same feeling was to be found among all those people who wished to modernize the old Russian Empire, including the Russian territories. They could not bear the ''dark people''; they considered peasants to be holding Russia back. Maxim Gorki speaks, for example, of his hope that the uncivilized, stupid people in the villages would die out; a new race of literate, rational, energetic people would take their place. As it turned out, the "rational," "energetic" people made a worse hash of agriculture than the stupid, uncivilized ones.

The modernizers were deluded as well as cruel. The peasant with all his faults was producing more with his wooden plow in 1914, as Khrushchev publicly observed in 1953, than the half million tractors and the modern fields did thirty or forty years later. The modernizers thought, "How modern we are. The countryside can be turned into a factory. Everything is rational; agriculture can be planned." They knew nothing about agriculture. They were totally uninformed. The planning idea resulted in ridiculous notions. By 1932, for example, the whole staff of the meteorological office had been arrested on the charge of falsifying weather forecasts in order to damage the harvest. The forecasters should have gotten their predictions right; it is a scientific matter. Marxists can always be scientific.

The other Marxist-Leninist doctrine that caused damage was simply the notion of class struggle, which Lenin introduced into the villages. Everything must proceed by class war. As a result, any villages that lacked class struggle had to find some. The peasants were therefore divided into kulaks, middle peasants, and poor peasants and laborers. The term "kulak" as it was used by the Communists was utterly spurious. The kulak was, in its original meaning, the moneylender, the grasping figure in the villages. This was not, however, an accurate description of prosperous peasants, and all the poor peasants of course tried to become prosperous.

The first wave of prosperous peasants was wiped out in 1917–1921. In 1921–1922 with the advent of the New Economic Policy (NEP), when the peasants had temporarily defeated the government, they began to have freedom to operate on the land and in the market, and of course a new lot of "kulaks" emerged. The poor peasant who worked hard became richer, so he became a kulak. Then, after the dekulakization of such people, many of whom had successfully fought in the Red Army, there were no longer any kulaks. There was no longer a stratum that fitted any of the old definitions of class. But the Party held that the kulak still existed though he could no longer be defined. Moreover it invented the category of "subkulak," which could be applied to any peasant.

Then, too, as James Mace will develop at greater length, Stalin and the Bolshevik leaders felt a hatred for the Ukrainian nation as a troublemaker. Jim Mace has aptly remarked that the position of Ukraine in the 1920s was rather like that of Poland with regard to Moscow today. The local Communists were not reliable; the Bolsheviks had to use local left-wing Social Revolutionaries. The Bolshevik regime had no roots except in the slightly Russianized cities, and it had to make concessions to Ukrainianization, as Jim Mace will note. They did not like making these concessions any more than they liked making concessions to the peasantry or accepting the New Economic Policy. And the result was a "Ukrainianization" which produced a great flowering of Ukrainian culture.

Now, I have spoken of motivation in a general sense where the Bolsheviks are concerned, but we are not accustomed to great events depending on attitudes and dogmas. We think in terms of social

5

forces, not crazy doctrines that lead people to take action for irrational reasons. We may ask what rationale there can possibly be for ruining the countryside, for half destroying a people, or for reducing the fields to nettles and thistles. From our point of view, there can be none; yet Stalin pursued a course that in one respect has not been uncommon in history if we look far enough back. No one wondered why Genghis Khan laid waste an area, why the Mongols destroyed the agriculture of Mesopotamia. This was common practice even for Wallenstein in the Thirty Years' War. Conquerors lay waste the countryside, kill a lot of people, take the crops, perhaps burn the villages.

Such a strategy, pursued for reasons of power, is not irrational. It has adverse economic results—in particular, when it ruins a great agricultural country—but it is not irrational as a way of imposing the will of the victorious party and crushing the nationhood and the peasantry of a country. Peasantry and nationality are related matters. As Dr. Dalrymple will no doubt mention, Stalin on several occasions expressed the view that the peasantry stands at the center of nationalism.

The peasant Ukrainian-speaking populace was the great force of nationality. During the famine, Ukrainian leaders time and time again said that they were crushing the kulaks, a bastion of nationalism. They simultaneously crushed the Ukrainian culture and the Ukrainian Independent church. They were crushing the Ukrainian nationality not only physically but also spiritually and culturally. We must see the picture in its entirety.

Michael Novak commented that the famine has not properly entered the consciousness of the West or of the world generally. In this connection we should consider Stalin's responsibility. Stalin was a much more devious man than Hitler. Even now, there are people who say, "Ah, but perhaps he didn't know," or "After all it's a famine, famines happen—natural events." It must be proved that this one was artificial. He never admitted that there was a famine, just as he never admitted that the Moscow trials were faked. He pretended he thought the accused were guilty. Stalin's direct knowledge and responsibility are clear. First of all, the Ukrainian Communists tried to have the disastrous grain deliveries reduced in August 1932 and were prevented from doing so. Then several of his leading people, such as Molotov and Kaganovich, went to the disaster areas. We also know that high officials approached him, for example a leading Ukrainian Communist, Terekhov, is quoted in *Pravda*, in 1964, as having said to him directly, "There is a famine in the Ukraine." Stalin is quoted as replying, "No, there isn't, you're a fantasist, go and join the union of writers." Indeed, Stalin's wife told him about it; she knew various students who had seen it. He knew perfectly well there was a famine. He wanted a famine. We can return to this important point later.

The other major point that we should consider concerns the death toll. I think we should briefly discuss the derivation of the figure of 7 million, which naturally does not represent 100 percent accuracy but is a soundly based general estimate. In the past it has been difficult to find accurate data. The census of 1937 was suppressed, and the census takers were all shot. A new, fake census, more satisfactory to the authorities, was produced in 1939. From material being published in the Soviet Union, however, we can now deduce the true figures of the suppressed census.

We now know that between 1926 and 1937 there was a population deficit of about 14 or 15 million. If we exclude 2 or 3 million babies unborn because their parents were no longer around, we have a figure of 11 or 12 million unnaturally dead. This estimate includes both the dekulakization and the famine, and it is not possible to determine how the deficit is divided between the two. Even if we disregard the 1937 census, however, and accept the faked 1939 census, we find that Ukraine then had only slightly more than 28 million people, far fewer than it had had in 1926. If the Ukrainian population had increased in the same proportion as the rest of the Soviet Union, the figure would have been higher by 7.8 million. Now, some of that missing increment would of course have been Ukrainians lost in the dekulakization, and, as I noted earlier, the 1939 census is wrong, probably exaggerating the Ukrainian population by 800,000 to a million. (In general, we are also omitting peasants who were in labor camps in 1935 and who later died; there were probably about 4 million of these people from the whole Soviet Union, so perhaps a million from Ukraine died in the camps during the next period.)

Finally, we may ask why the famine has been forgotten. First, as I have noted, Stalin was devious and clever and managed to evade responsibility. He denied that there was a famine, but it is not true that it was not reported in the West. Many of the Western papers—*Figaro*, the *Manchester Guardian*, some of the American papers—reported it fully. Many of the great papers printed perfectly clear reports. The famine was not suppressed by the press, but Stalin persuaded Édouard Herriot, Sir John Maynard, and other well-known people to go to the Potemkin villages and declare that there was no famine. As a result the man in the street could say, "Oh, well, perhaps there isn't a famine; perhaps this is just propaganda. Stalin denies it; you've got to prove it." Second, of course, there was the left in general, laying the odds in favor of the Soviet Union. George Orwell remarked that momentous events such as the Ukrainian famine are simply not known, are suppressed in the minds of people who are pro-Soviet. Third, the idea that Ukraine was a nation, that its people had national feelings, had not established itself in the West as Polish nationhood had done, simply because Ukraine had had only very brief periods of independence. It had never become a nation in Western eyes, and as a result it wasn't clear that there was a people against whom Stalin could commit an act.

I do not know whether anybody in particular can be blamed for such sheer ignorance. Nowadays we are in a better position. Western economists about ten years ago started writing about the whole peasant problem in a way that no longer presupposed rationality of the type that economists have been inclined to attribute to Stalin. Much research has now been done, and much piecemeal information is available in the Soviet Union. We are unlikely to forget the famine again. Michael Novak referred earlier to the killing of 269 people. A Ukrainian friend of mine observed that to match the slaughter that occurred in Ukraine, it would be necessary to shoot down an airliner with 269 passengers every day for seventy-five years. I will leave you with that thought.

James Mace

Let me first mention the size of the area of which we are speaking. Soviet Ukraine today is about as large as France. The Soviet Ukraine of 1933 was somewhat smaller because perhaps a quarter of the country to the west was then under Polish rule. According to the Soviet census of 1926, which seems to have been a good one, there were 31.2 million Ukrainians in the Soviet Union. In 1939, according to the very inadequate census we have from that year, which is actually only a slim, one-volume summary, there were only 28.1 million Ukrainians in the Soviet Union. Comparison of the figures gives us an absolute drop of 3.1 million Ukrainians.

Now, Ukrainian statistical journals in the 1920s and early 1930s included administrative estimates of the natural growth rate of the population as late as 1931. Using these rates, we find that in 1931 there should have been 34.2 million Ukrainians, assuming that the growth rate figures are correct. If we take the rate of population growth shown by the Ukrainians in the late 1950s and work backward from the number of Ukrainians in 1939, we can estimate that there were only 26.3 million Ukrainians in 1934. So the difference between our estimates of the 1934 population of Ukrainians and the 1931 number of Ukrainians in the Soviet Union amounts to 7.9 million. About 200,000 Ukrainian families were dekulakized and exiled. We can assume that about a quarter of a million people probably died in the very harsh circumstances of exile, so we can subtract a quarter of a million right there. If we allow another 100,000 or 200,000 Ukrainians for the purges, we still have a figure of more than 7 million people who died unnaturally, probably because of famine. That figure accounts for about half of all the unnatural deaths in the Soviet Union during the period.

The reason why so many Ukrainians perished becomes clearer when we turn to some recently published research by a Soviet immigrant demographer who writes under the name Maksudov on the geography of the famine of 1933. He has analyzed the age structure of rural females by oblast (region) in the 1959 population. He shows that

9

since there is a lower birth rate and since infants tend to die first in famine conditions, there is a trough in the age structure corresponding to the famine. This trough—demographic evidence of massive mortality in this period—appears in fifteen of the sixteen oblasts of Soviet Ukraine, except in the far north, where there are a number of streams and more people were probably able to survive, by fishing or whatever, and throughout the Kuban, which certainly at that time was considered a non-Russian area. There were more than 3 million Ukrainians in the Kuban, according to the 1926 census. Only about 150,000 Ukrainians remain there today. In addition, the Kuban Cossacks, who had tried to set up their own state at the time of the Russian Revolution, were a strong, nationally self-assertive population that in its way can be seen as having threatened the Soviet Union somewhat as Ukrainians did. Finally, there is spotty evidence of unnatural mortality during the same period in the Volga region. As we know, the Volga Germans were later exiled en masse. We do not know as much about the Volga as we know about Ukraine and the Kuban.

To understand why millions of people died in these particular areas we must realize that the Bolsheviks hated not only the peasantry, not only nationalities, but basically everything that did not fit into their blueprint for restructuring society. In 1921, with the adoption of the New Economic Policy, the Bolsheviks momentarily ceased their attempt to restructure society completely. In 1928, with the beginning of the cultural revolution, and in 1929, with the beginning of collectivization, the Bolsheviks were in a sense once again trying to finish business remaining from the civil war period—that is, they were basically trying to eliminate everything they did not like in society. The things they did not like included the peasantry, the so-called bourgeois intelligentsia, and any nationally self-assertive national groups.

To understand why Ukrainians were perceived to be a threat, we must go back in time to the 1920s. The Ukrainians had declared their independence in January 1918; Ukrainian governments had managed to survive territorially until 1921. In 1923, the Bolsheviks adopted a policy called indigenization, or "taking root," as a way of coping with Ukrainians and other national groups. The Russian word is *korenizatsiia*. The new policy was designed to confer a veneer of national legitimacy on the regimes that the Bolsheviks had established in the so-called border lands. In the Ukrainian case the policy worked too well. Prominent Ukrainian national leaders started to return from exile. The most prominent was the first president of Independent Ukraine, Mykhailo Hrushevsky, who came back to the Ukrainian Academy of

Sciences, edited a historical journal, and worked on his *History of Ukraine-Rus,* probably the centerpiece of Ukrainian scholarship. Creative national energies burst forth, and Ukrainian writers flourished.

Ukraine is a nation whose very language had been illegal in the Russian Empire from 1876 until 1905. It was very difficult to publish anything even in the years after 1905. In the 1920s, when the fetters had been taken off, there was an unprecedented cultural flowering that began to affect the Ukrainian party organization, the Communist party of Ukraine. Now as Mr. Conquest has observed, Moscow could not trust the local organization in Ukraine. Ukrainian Communists in the 1920s were arguing that it was time for a Ukrainian to be first secretary of the Communist party of Ukraine, that Stalin should withdraw the lieutenant who held that particular post at the time, that Ukraine should emancipate itself from Russian cultural influence, and that Ukraine was being exploited economically by the Soviet Union and by Moscow. Stalin in particular found these demands very difficult to accept. In 1928 he was finally forced to compromise with the Ukrainian organization. In order to defeat Bukharin, he needed the support of the largest Soviet party organization, which happened to be the Ukrainian organization. To secure it he withdrew Kaganovich and allowed the Ukrainians to chart their own course for a time. A political strongman emerged, a sort of Gomulka figure named Mykola Skrypnyk.

Soon after Stalin had defeated Bukharin, he began a sort of political siege against Skrypnyk. With the beginning of the cultural revolution on an all-union stage, we see, in the Ukrainian political arena, the fall of Skrypnyk's political clients and ideological watchdogs. The major Communist Ukrainian historian of the period, for example, is condemned and purged for—and this is quite interesting—treating the history of Ukraine as a distinct process, for asserting that Ukrainian history is different from Russian history and is a legitimate field of study. Removing this person produced a certain ideological provincialization of Ukraine within the Soviet context. In 1930 there was a massive purge of Ukrainian cultural and spiritual elites. The Ukrainian Autocephalous Orthodox church, which had been set up in 1917, was abolished in 1930. Many of its leaders went in the dock in a show trial involving something called the Union for the Liberation of Ukraine. At the same time, members of the Ukrainian Academy of Sciences were brought in, including people who had returned from exile in the 1920s, and were accused not only of plotting to assassinate Stalin—of leading a rebellion—but also of attempting sabotage by giving words a spelling that differed from the Russian and by interpreting history in a certain way. People actually confessed to these crimes and were sent into the Gulag. These political developments culminated in the great famine of 1933.

Now, as Bob Conquest mentioned, Ukrainian officials in 1932 were going to Moscow, telling Stalin and anyone who would listen that people were starving to death. There is even a passage in *Khrushchev Remembers* where Khrushchev recalled that Demchenko, one of the oblast secretaries in Ukraine, had come to Mikoyan saying that the trains were pulling into Kiev loaded with dead bodies that had been picked up all along the route. Stalin knew what was going on. He took the opportunity to accuse the Ukrainian organization of criminal laxity in failing to meet the grain quotas, and he took charge. He sent in another satrap, this time a man called Postyshev, ostensibly to make sure that the grain quotas were met. They could not be met; people were already starving to death, so obviously no crops remained in the countryside. The grain procurement brigades went around once again with their long pointed sticks and tried to find hidden supplies. In addition, Stalin and Postyshev started a campaign against Ukrainian bourgeois nationalism. In March 1933 Skrypnyk was demoted, and in June he was denounced by name. Postyshev announced that the agricultural problems reflected insufficient vigilance; Skrypnyk was charged with having hidden nationalistic deviationists and wreckers—people responsible for failure to meet the grain quotas. Skrypnyk was purged and driven to suicide.

To understand the Ukrainian famine, in other words, we must view it not only in the context of collectivization but also in terms of political developments. Let us consider why the people died where they did. Let us look at the famine in a different context. The peasantry, the social basis of the Ukrainian nation, was more than decimated. The nation lost 7 million people. Ukrainianization ended, paving the way for the eventual re-Russification of the cities in eastern and central Ukraine. The spiritual and cultural elites were destroyed. In 1930, 259 Ukrainian writers were publishing in Soviet Ukraine. By 1938, only 36 of them continued to publish—in other words, more than 80 percent were eliminated in this period. The Ukrainian intelligentsia was destroyed; the official national Communist leadership was destroyed. The famine was thus not only the outcome of collectivization but also an important tactic in nationality policy, an attempt by the Soviet regime to solve its Ukrainian problem once and for all.

Dana Dalrymple

In speaking today, I will be presenting my own personal views. As a government employee I enjoy being called a scholar, and I certainly am delighted to take part in today's discussion. In a sense I have waited twenty years for this day. When I first started investigating the famine, there was no community of scholars and no opportunity for a session of this sort. On the other hand, I did not anticipate that twenty years would pass before interest in the famine built to its present level, but fiftieth anniversaries do have a way of bringing matters into sharper focus.

Articles that have recently appeared in the Ukrainian press have aptly called it the *great* famine. It was real, vast, and terrible—and it was of course basically man-made. Jim Mace has spoken of the famine's impact on Ukraine, but it of course had far broader consequences. Virtually all of the southeastern Soviet Union seems to have been caught up in it in one way or another, and of course some Ukrainians lived in these areas. Thus we need to raise our estimates of the mortality. Jim Mace gave the figure of 7 million; to this we should add an unknown number of deaths elsewhere in the southern part of the Soviet Union.

As today's other speakers have indicated, the famine was virtually unknown at the time despite the vast mortality and despite the fact that a number of accounts were published. Curiously, general histories of the Soviet Union still make little mention of the famine. In retrospect, the famine certainly seems to represent one of the most successful news management stories in history. It seems incredible now that Stalin could have pulled off such a feat.

Still, as we have seen, it is possible to assemble basic information about the famine, and many more pieces have become available in recent years. Differing perspectives on the famine can be taken. We might look at the famine solely in Ukraine, where of course it was the worst. In my article "The Soviet Famine of 1932–34," I took a somewhat broader perspective. I will continue to do so, but irrespective of geographic focus, the basic story of the famine is much the same: It was a man-made event producing widespread mortality and involving a cover-up by the government.

Let us consider the background for disaster. Several basic tenets guided Soviet policy toward agriculture. Moshe Lewin mentioned the special importance of grain. He wrote: "During the so-called era of the first Five-Year Plans in the Soviet Union, and indeed during the whole of Stalin's rule, grain (and ways of securing it) played a crucial role in the Soviet system. It was a strategic raw material indispensable to the process of running the state and industrializing it."[2] In addition, the Soviet leaders were, of course, motivated by a basic desire to control the countryside. The tools for this process, which have already been mentioned were principally collectivization and dekulakization.

The collectivization process was facilitated by mechanization, which played a curious role. The Soviets regarded tractors as giving them a way to achieve the modern capitalist type of agriculture that they wanted in some ways. Yet the process of collectivization was both helped and hindered by mechanization. Collectivization brought about the killing of much livestock, which increased the need for mechanization. The problem was that the Soviets had few tractors and virtually no tractor industry. They therefore had to import tractors and the wherewithal to build plants. Both steps increased the need for procurement from the countryside to pay the costs of foreign exchange. So one problem fed on the other.

The procurement system seems to have been the major direct factor in bringing about the famine. The government under the five-year plans had relied on procurements for exports partly to pay for industrialization and partly to import the tractors. Procurement was also made for domestic purposes, for cities, for factories, and particularly for the military. As Lewin noted, "The Politburo . . . supervised closely all the stages of the campaign and constantly intervened in it. For a good quarter of a century, extracting grain from the peasants amounted to a permanent state of warfare against them and was understood as such by both sides."[3] Grossman stated the matter even more succinctly: "I came to understand that the main thing for the Soviet power is the Plan. Fulfill the Plan."[4]

As a result, the situation in the countryside by 1931–1932 was

---

2. Moshe Lewin, "'Taking Grain': Soviet Policies of Agricultural Procurements before the War," in C. Abramsky, ed. (assisted by B. J. Williams), *Essays in Honour of E.H. Carr* (London: MacMillan, 1974), p. 281.

3. Ibid., 281–82.

4. Vasily Grossman, as cited by Adam B. Ulam, *Stalin, The Man and His Era* (New York: Viking Press, 1973), p. 346. The quotation is taken from the Russian text of *Forever Flowing*, published in West Germany in 1970, p. 123.

largely a disaster. Collectivization had resulted in mass disorganization, mass resistance among the peasants, and the destruction of livestock. The machinery on which the Soviets had placed so much emphasis was breaking down, and they did not know how to repair and maintain it. Agricultural production was a shambles, in short.

At the same time, procurement levels showed continued growth from the mid-1920s. It is possible in part that some misinformation may have been involved. Grossman made an interesting comment on this subject. He wrote:

> After the liquidation of the kulaks, the amount of land under cultivation dropped very sharply and so did the crop yield. But meanwhile people continued to report that without the kulaks our whole life was flourishing. The village soviet lied to the district, and the district lied to the province, and the province lied to Moscow. Everything was apparently in order, so Moscow assigned grain production and delivery quotas to the provinces, and the provinces then assigned them to the districts. And our village was given a quota that it couldn't have fulfilled in ten years! In the village soviet, even those who weren't drinkers took to drink out of terror.[5]

The results were predictable. Production dropped in 1931, and the procurement level increased. The increase in the procurement level seems to have been made possible by the drop in livestock numbers, which reduced the amount of grain used for livestock feed.

In retrospect, collectivization was really a massive failure, and indeed Miller suggests that there was a net inflow of material products into agriculture during the first Five Year Plan.[6] During the period, then, collectivization did not provide a substantial source of economic growth for the country; instead it was a burden. Because of the poor agricultural production, the procurement process imposed an even greater burden.

The events of the 1932–1933 crop year were also then fairly predictible. There was once again a short crop, though not a disastrous one, and procurements continued at a high level, but not as high as in the previous year, largely because the cupboard was bare. In addition, some produce may have been directed into the private market, where prices were much higher. The response by the government was pre-

---

5. Vasily Grossman, *Forever Flowing*, trans. Thomas P. Whitney (New York: Harper and Row, 1972), p. 149.

6. James R. Millar, "Mass Collectivization and the Contribution of Soviet Agriculture to the First Five-Year Plan: A Review Article," *Slavic Review* (December 1974), pp. 759–66.

dictable: It increased terror in the procurement process. The result was famine. The situation during 1933–1934 was somewhat the same but less severe. The famine clearly was man-made.

The Soviet government perhaps inadvertently set the stage but then did nothing to avert the famine. The government could certainly have lessened the severity of the famine, and could perhaps avoided it, by relaxing procurements. It could have reduced grain exports— they did not play such a major role in the foreign trade situation. The government could have used some of its own stocks, those that had been established for the military, to alleviate famine. The Soviets could have gone further, importing grain. They could even have allowed outside famine relief. As we know, they did none of these things. The big question is why, and the answer inevitably involves Stalin.

Clearly Stalin did not have a good attitude toward the peasants; they had resisted his efforts at collectivization. They also threatened the sanctity of the plan and of the procurement process. He presumably desired to conceal the fact of the famine for the sake of prestige and possibly for diplomatic reasons. The Soviets were trying to gain U.S. recognition at the time, and they also sought admission into the League of Nations. Then, too, Stalin had a malignant nature, which Dr. Conquest has eloquently described.

Does the information now available justify the recently leveled charge of Ukrainian genocide? The answer is debatable. The general events that I have described, particularly collectivization and procurement, took place throughout the Soviet Union. Many of the actions that we hear about in Ukraine were also taken in Smolensk, for example, although with far less disastrous results in terms of human lives.[7] Famine, as I indicated earlier, occurred over a wide area of the southern part of the Soviet Union. Events of course were most severe in Ukraine, which was the breadbasket and the area where resistance was greatest. As Grossman wrote: "It was clear that Moscow was basing its hopes on the Ukraine. And the upshot of it was that most of the subsequent anger was directed against the Ukraine."[8]

Some observers would view the events in Ukraine as the most terrible chapter in a larger story, but it may be that the coincidence of the famine and other forms of repression against the Ukrainians warrant the more severe charge of genocide. Perhaps in the discussion Drs. Conquest and Mace will address this question further.

---

7. Daniel R. Brower, "Collectivized Agriculture in Smolensk: The Party, the Peasantry, and the Crisis of 1932," *The Russian Review* (April 1977), pp. 151–66.
8. Grossman, *Forever Flowing*, p. 149.

Virtually all our information, however, is from the outside. We have essentially no inside official or semiofficial documentation from Soviet archives. If Soviet documents exist, there is probably no chance that they will ever be revealed. Public memoirs are not common in the Soviet Union, and in this case it seems unlikely that Stalin would have said anything about the famine.[9] Thus our knowledge of the famine, as overwhelming as it is, is incomplete and is likely to remain so.

In future assessments of the famine, it would probably be useful to broaden the scope of research beyond Ukraine to encompass the whole area of famine. It is to be hoped that the efforts now under way, and possibly other work yet to be undertaken, will bring to light the full story of this terrible period in Soviet history.

---

9. Khrushchev's memoirs are an exception. He provided only a brief reference to the famine. See *Khrushchev Remembers* (Boston: Little, Brown, 1970), p. 74.

Discussion

MR. NOVAK: The shooting down of the Korean airliner has caused greater outrage than the immense man-made famine of 1933 partly because it is relatively easy to imagine a planeload of people. We have all been on airplanes; we can imagine what the experience involved. Furthermore, it is very difficult to penetrate a closed society. If 269 peasants and their children in a single village had been annihilated on September 1, 1933, we would perhaps be more readily shocked. Alternatively, if 100,000 people in Ukraine—or 400,000 or 1 million— had been starved to death deliberately in 1933, our horror would be similarly immense. The larger the number, however, the harder it is to imagine. Yet psychologically it is crucial somehow to understand what it was like. Did survivors who were witnesses leave testimony describing the catastrophe for a given family? What material is available?

DR. CONQUEST: Much material has been produced in a number of books, edited mostly by members of the Ukrainian community. They tell story after story of village after village and family after family. There is some variation, as Jim Mace notes. Areas with fish fared better than areas without, and if woods with acorns were nearby, people fared better than they would have otherwise. Certain areas were slightly better off than others. Some villages saw total destruction; nobody was left at all. There are quite a number of accounts by people who looked in and saw the last dead child lying on the floor or clasped to the breast of its dead mother. I must have read between 500 and 1,000 such accounts at least, and probably more exist.

MR. NOVAK: One that particularly gripped me concerned a young girl of about four who asked her father to come with her to visit her friend because the other child's father had taken the friend away in a mood she did not understand. They went and found no one in the cottage of the friend's family, but as the man moved behind the door, he felt what turned out to be the body of a child hanging, saliva dripping on the chest, and then discovered that the father had hanged the younger daughter too. The dead children were ten and eleven, and

18

the visitor fled in terror with his young daughter, thinking that they might be murdered too. When they met the father of the dead children, he begged them, beseeched them, not to tell his wife, who was away on a two-day trip looking for food. She had been feeding the children, and he was starving. He feared for his life and feared for the misery of the children; he would even have hanged the third child. The man had, the account says, gone mad with hunger. Is there a collection of these stories that we might mention?

DR. MACE: There are a number of them. When Ukrainian survivors first immigrated after the war, one organization published much material of this kind, often in rather imperfect English. The organization is called Dobrus, a Ukrainian acronym for the Democratic Association of Ukrainians who had been suppressed by the Soviets. Dobrus published in 1953 and 1955 a collection of eyewitness documents called the *Black Deeds of the Kremlin*, perhaps not the best title but certainly conveying what the Ukrainians felt. It included hundreds of stories. Dobrus and other organizations also put out a number of collections in the Ukrainian language. *Black Deeds* is probably the most available and complete.

In addition there are numerous unpublished eyewitness accounts, a hitherto fairly untapped resource. In the early 1950s, Harvard University in conjunction with the U.S. Air Force carried out a project to interview people who had recently immigrated during the war from the Soviet Union. About a third of the people interviewed by Harvard University refugee interview project were Ukrainians, and they all had famine stories to tell. There were many of them, and the interviewers were not particularly interested in the famine. Notations appear in the transcripts, which still exist, that the interviewer just stopped the recorder when the respondent began talking about the famine of 1933. The person became very emotional, and the interviewer became very sympathetic. Once they had finished with the subject, the interviewer again started asking questions and recording. But there is much eyewitness material from such projects, and a number of individual accounts have also been published.

MR. NOVAK: What about the mobilization force itself? It must have been huge—including all the people who were sent to find, procure, and collect the food. Do we have any idea about the numbers or any accounts from participants?

DR. MACE: Yes, a campaign began in 1930 and called itself the Twenty-five Thousanders, and there were other campaigns of 10,000 and 5,000 people who were sent to the Soviet countryside initially to force the peasants into collective farms, to identify kulaks, to organize the local activists to go out and seize them, and to carry off their possessions and to throw them out of their houses. There were about 7,000 of these Twenty-five Thousanders in the Ukraine and who knows how many people with other titles, plenipotentiaries of the Central Committee and party workers, thousands of them. Now, in the Ukrainian case, most of the Thousanders of whom we have the greatest knowledge seem to have been non-Ukrainian workers. We have no nationality breakdown but find that the majority of these people were workers with more than ten years' seniority, which usually meant Russian or Russified. Under Ukrainianization, the situation resembled somewhat that which presently exists in Montreal: The character of Montreal is becoming more and more French, and English people who have lived in the city feel more and more foreign. Some of them are having trouble learning French.

The Ukrainian cities were pretty well Russified in eastern and central Ukraine at the time of the revolution. With Ukrainians coming in during the 1920s and with a policy favorable to Ukrainian language and culture, the character of the city began to change. So there was national antagonism, and many who volunteered to go into the countryside already had a grudge against Ukrainians. Many of the accounts mention so-and-so, a Thousander who came into a village and adopted the Russian slogan *vplot do pechenogo*, which literally means "even the baked"—that is, even if you see half a loaf of baked bread on the stove, you take that too. People were available who were quite eager to carry on this particular task. At the same time a great many Ukrainians were involved. The support organizations in the Ukrainian villages were of course composed of Ukrainians.

DR. CONQUEST: A very large number of books by defectors of every possible type describe experiences during the famine. Some people came from Ukraine or had been in Ukraine. In addition, many people worked as activists. Lev Kopelev, who is now in Washington, was a young Communist sent to the Ukrainian village, as were Leonid Plyushch and Kravchenko. There are many very good firsthand descriptions told from the point of view of the man who was working as a Communist in the villages. One remarkable aspect of these accounts is that they are all completely consistent with each other. Although one of them might initially seem exaggerated or invented, they complement each other to a very large degree. Grigorenko was also in Ukraine and wrote a book. As Jim Mace noted, the Young Communists and the Young Pioneers, the Leninist Boy Scout–age organization, were called out.

Children—25,000 of them—were used to guard the crops in Ukraine, not to guard them physically with rifles, but to watch them, to report to the police and to the military, and to raise the alarm. We have heard a horrible story of children being hanged by their father. There are many stories of a similar type, not necessarily quite the same, of people killing their children to end their misery or just turning them out of the house to fend for themselves. A mother is said to have abandoned a boy of six by the railway, saying he could manage better by joining a gang—and so on. I think one of the general horrors of the whole episode is that, for the most part, children under six or seven died. They could not manage. Children between, say, six or seven and about fourteen went off in large numbers to join gangs and became criminals. Others were rounded up in children's camps or just died. Still others were rounded up in yards and in railway wagons, guarded and not given enough to eat and starved. Some went to homes, and some trained as secret police officers. This group of children was a resource of the present secret police.

Although the physical sufferings of the children were intense, I think the spiritual suffering also deserves consideration. An American girl recently went to Russia and was taken to the Komsomol headquarters in Moscow where she was shown the statue of Pavlik Morozov. Pavlik Morozov denounced his father for hoarding grain. Thereafter the father suffered the fate of grain hoarders, and Pavlik, who was thirteen or fourteen years old, was killed by angry villagers and so became a martyr. I wonder whether it is worse to have children die with the family or go out and become Pavlik Morozovs. The regime has that crime on its conscience even more than the killing, in my view.

MR. NOVAK: What kept the peasants from fleeing? Was there a passport system?

DR. MACE: Yes, passportization, as it was called, was first introduced in late 1932 in Soviet Ukraine and at various times in various other parts of the Soviet Union. People who lived in cities or in certain border areas had to have a passport. The peasants therefore could not leave the land, and they could not live off the land. Passportization juridically tied the agricultural population to the land.

MR. NOVAK: That policy sounds like a reversion to serfdom.

DR. MACE: Very much so. In fact, it is not possible in Ukrainian, but in Russian some people used the party's initials, VKP, for the all-union

21

Communist party in Russia, to mean *vtoroe krepostnoe pravo*, "law of the second serfdom." They were looking at collectivization, which physically was very much like serfdom. It eliminated small private farms, creating large estates and tying the peasants to the land so that they could not leave. In addition, certain labor obligations were introduced in the 1930s for which workers were not paid—an arrangement similar to the French *corvée*. Second, in the Ukrainian case, there were efforts to prevent villagers from leaving the republic and to prevent people from carrying food in, even bagmen: A person carrying a sack of potatoes was not allowed to cross the border. The Soviets stopped the trains at the border, according to numerous eyewitness accounts, including some from people who were at that time in fairly high positions. Guards would seize any food found on the train, and the person carrying it was usually arrested on charges of speculation, an offense that carried the death penalty. At the same time, the railroads were forbidden to sell tickets to Russia to people who obviously came from the Ukrainian villages.

MR. NOVAK: In other words, the wagons went into the village to take all the grain that could be found. Searchers went into houses, barns, sheds, and even fields. Then, in addition, food could not be brought in.

DR. MACE: Right. That is precisely what happened.

DR. CONQUEST: This supports Dr. Dalrymple's theory about the localization of the famine. Not only were peasants not allowed out to find food, but when they did leave, they were not allowed to return with food. A physical blockade prevented anybody from bringing even a few loaves into Ukraine. This is a clear sign that there was a definite intention to localize the famine in Ukraine, and there was no famine on the other side. Naturally, no one in Russia was living well after collectivization, but the grain requisitions in other areas were not physically destructive, though the Russians to the north in fact lived in a more rural, not a less rural, area than Ukraine. Between 1926 and 1939—I am using the official figures, and in both cases there may be some slight error—the Ukrainians went down by 9.9 percent, the Byelorussians went up by 11.3 percent. There is total difference on either side of that border.

MR. NOVAK: It is about 20 percent.

DR. CONQUEST: The Russians went up by 28 percent in this period when the Ukrainians were going down by maybe 10 percent. It was not localized totally in Ukraine; there were other areas which suffered, but the Kuban was largely Ukrainian speaking and the inhabitants considered themselves Ukrainian. But the famine also raged in the lower Volga: The Volga Germans were mainly Mennonites and Evangelicals, very strongly so, like some of the Amish. Their 100,000 letters to the West went to Lutheran and other organizations, and some of these letters were published. I have no figures for the Germans, and it is very difficult to determine what happened, but the stories are much the same. I have not, indeed, come across cannibalism stories, though.

There was much cannibalism in Ukraine. We have a decree or instruction by the deputy head of the Ukrainian secret police saying that there was nothing in the penal law against cannibalism. Of course there was nothing. You would not find anything in American law against cannibalism. So the official declared that cannibalism should be regarded as a state crime. Suspects were arrested by the secret police, and cannibals were usually shot. Still, as Vasily Grossman observes, Who caused women to eat their children? They were driven mad.

MR. NOVAK: Could you say a few words about the question of inadvertence and deliberate intent? If there was a blockade, if there was a large-scale mobilization, if the initial decree was impossible and punitive in its very structure, can we still speak of inadvertence?

DR. CONQUEST: Well, it would involve the life or death of 20 percent of a people. The margin seems to me to be too great to be dismissed in that way.

MR. NOVAK: Why didn't Stalin or someone else appeal to the American Relief Administration—a famine relief agency headed by Herbert Hoover—which had been so successful in the very early days of the revolution within Russia itself?

DR. CONQUEST: That question contains its own answer. The Soviets did not want the famine to be coped with successfully.

DR. MACE: Even in the case of the ARA, it's significant that the initial request for relief was solely for the Volga. Efforts were made for a while to keep relief from Ukraine quite simply because food was perceived to be a weapon.

MR. NOVAK: My point was that the ARA was an available precedent.

DR. MACE: Certainly, the precedent was there. What was not there was the desire to use it.

MR. NOVAK: Describe the picture as journalists saw it. Malcolm Muggeridge is justly famous for his honesty at the time. What did a person see who traveled by train or went into the villages as an outsider?

DR. MACE: At every train station, first of all, people were lying down, begging, and people died. The train stations were literally overflowing with people. The peasants tried to flee to train stations.

MR. NOVAK: To make contact with the outside world?

DR. MACE: Right. Some villages totally died out and became deserted. One great Russian engineer was sent in, I believe it was into the north Caucasus, the Kuban, to inspect wells, and she entered a village that had completely died out. She speaks of the stench and some of the scenes she saw. In every village there were people who had swollen from hunger. Literally everyone in the village swelled with starvation. Bodies lay in the street, even in the cities. Photographs published in the 1930s show Kharkov, then the capital of Soviet Ukraine, with dead bodies on the street and people walking past them because corpses had become an everyday sight by that time. In the villages, the situation was of course much worse, and it was no longer even possible to give people decent burials. Bodies were just loaded on a wagon that went around.

MR. NOVAK: Are there collective graves?

DR. MACE: Mass graves? Yes, there are.

MR. NOVAK: Are there collections of photographs in existence?

DR. MACE: Yes, I think there is one collection in the Longworth Building that was part of the exhibit recently held in Cannon House Office Building.

MR. NOVAK: How complete is the photographic record?

DR. MACE: There are two principal sources of photographs. An American journalist, Thomas Walker, published photographs in the old Hearst press in 1935. The Hearst press covered the story rather tardily because Hearst became angry with Roosevelt in 1935, but a great many of the photographs were published in the Hearst chain—in the *New York American*, the *Evening Journal*, and the *Chicago American*.

MR. NOVAK: Didn't the United States first learn of the famine in 1934?

DR. MACE: The year was 1933, I believe. The second source of photographs is the German-language edition of Ewald Ammende's *Muss Russland Hungern*. The English translation, *Human Life in Russia*, took some photographs from the Walker account and omitted some that appeared in the German edition, which was published in Vienna in 1935. Most of the photos that I have seen come from these two sources.

MR. NOVAK: I understand from a comment made earlier that we have reports from people who participated in the mobilization. Were there widespread feelings of guilt? Do the participants still have latent feelings of guilt?

DR. CONQUEST: My impression is that most of the participants at the time, or at least all of those about whom I read, adopted an attitude like that of the gas chamber operators. They had convinced themselves, as Grossman notes, that the kulak was not human. Grossman, who was himself a Jew, makes the comparison. Just as the Germans felt that the Jew was not human, so the participants learned that a kulak was not human. Second, the participants were carrying out orders even if they had to brace themselves to kill people; it was the will of history. Even Mikhail Sholokhov, the Kremlin's favorite novelist, writes of how poor and defenseless the kulak family was, and he has Communist activists who cannot and will not do their fearful job. This is what Bukharin meant, I think, when he said that the party had become brutalized by the killing of men, women, and children who had done nothing; once Communists started wavering, the party got rid of them. Such people were purged on a very large scale. They could not bear to continue, but some of the people, like Kopelev, at the time thought, "It's a bit odd, but this is what the party says. The party is always right; history is cruel." He did not feel the shock at the time, and now he does.

MR. NOVAK: Did the famine intimidate? Is there a noticeable scar on the population, perhaps visible even much later, where the famine was concentrated? Part of Ukraine was in Polish hands at the time. Is there a detectable pattern of intimidation?

25

DR. MACE: Certainly the traditional centers of Ukrainian nationalism and self-assertion were Kiev and Poltava. I think most people would say that now the main center of Ukrainian activism outside the city of Kiev is Galicia, which was under Poland at the time of the famine in Soviet Ukraine. Now, the people who did the Soviets' bidding were also intimidated. The Soviet Ukrainian newspapers during the period carried editorials against "opportunists" who did not want to see the kulaks in their midst. Local officials were being removed right and left; hundreds of collective farm managers and thousands of members of the boards running collective farms were purged. Their fate is unknown but is fairly easy to imagine. There was certainly a sword of Damocles hanging over the heads of the people who were carrying out party instructions as well. As for the Ukrainians, I think it really did crush them for a number of years. In the Second World War the Ukrainian insurrectionary army (UPA), center of Ukrainian resistance activity, was based in western Ukraine, not in eastern Ukraine.

MR. NOVAK: Is the famine remembered in Ukraine today? Are there signs of bitterness?

DR. MACE: There are some. Vitaly Shevchenko, a Ukrainian political prisoner, for example, was sentenced for anti-Soviet agitation and propaganda—among other things, for mentioning the famine. People who come out, former dissidents and the like with whom I have spoken, state that the younger generation has appallingly little knowledge of the famine. The older generation knows about it but is often afraid to speak; it is something people do not really want to remember, a very traumatic experience. People never hear about it in the schools. People who were educated during the Khrushchev period found small mentions in the books of things like great errors and abuses. Professor Conquest has, I believe, some extracts from a Soviet demography textbook stating that progress toward lower mortality rates was not linear, that there were setbacks, and that the harvest failure of 1932 in Ukraine probably caused a very temporary rise in the mortality rate.

DR. CONQUEST: This mention appears in a Soviet demographic work three or four years old. In judging the various data and discussing the lowering of the death rate during the creation of socialism, the authors said that certain areas of the country did not keep pace. "The 1930 decrease in the number of cattle in Kazakhstan, for example, and the crop failure of 1932 in Ukraine may even have given rise to a temporary increase in mortality." This is not what you might call a very great admission.

DR. MACE: There are mentions of things like a "severe shortfall in edible produce" that caused "difficulties." Some Soviet fictional literature deals with the famine. Soviet Union fiction, or what purports to be fiction, can actually be much truer than that which purports to be history, because only in fiction is it possible to talk about some things. It is almost impossible to talk now about what happened in Soviet Ukraine, but a few writers can mention what went on in the Volga, where the situation seems to have been not quite as bad. I believe Mikhael Alexeev recently published a novel in the mass circulation *Roman Gazeta* about the famine, and he was in fact a famine survivor from the Volga region. A few years earlier he was able to publish a brief autobiography in the journal *Nash Sovremennik* (no. 9, 1972) in which he mentioned the traumatic experience of seeing his parents' coffins being carried away. In Ukraine and in the Kuban—I hate to sound callous—there were no coffins simply because too many people were dying. This was death on a different order of magnitude.

MR. NOVAK: There are euphemistic treatments in the more or less classic books of Russian history that are assigned reading for a liberal education today. The work of E. H. Carr is one example. Have any Soviet official texts, encyclopedias, or other books gone further, offering at least a vague description?

DR. CONQUEST: As far as I know, there is no reference whatever to the famine in any encyclopedia or any reference book of that sort.

MR. NOVAK: Is there a total blank?

DR. MACE: It is not total; we are not saying that there has never been a slight mention.

DR. CONQUEST: Still, it is pretty small.

DR. MACE: We searched far to find the example we gave, which is not very much.

MR. NOVAK: In other words, can we say that this audience has been privileged to hear freshly translated one of the most explicit admissions?

DR. CONQUEST: I think that it was explicit. The Soviets are cracking down on people who speak of the famine, the fiction writers. In the last eighteen months or so, they have been in trouble.

MR. NOVAK: Was there then and for a time thereafter, and is there now, some effect that this famine has exerted on agriculture in the Soviet Union?

DR. DALRYMPLE: There certainly was an effect at the time, but just how long it lingered is hard to say.

MR. NOVAK: Can we see this effect in figures for cattle and grain, for example?

DR. DALRYMPLE: Yes, it is true for each. The famine was sometimes more severe in areas where there was monoculture in grain; families could not fall back on a diversified agriculture. The draft cattle had been killed and were no longer available for slaughter. Once the grain was gone, nothing remained. Many years passed before the livestock numbers increased in the Soviet Union. They may not really have recovered until the 1940s or later. Grain production of course recovered faster, but then we have only the Soviet statistics for grain production, which may not be accurate. In addition, the biological unit of yield was introduced sometime after the famine.

MR. NOVAK: What was that?

DR. CONQUEST: It began in 1933, I think. The biological yield was denounced by Khrushchev in 1953. For a biological yield, rather than counting the actual grain collected, people estimate it in the field. Someone looks at a field and says that is has fifty tons of grain. The real amount is determined later. According to Khrushchev, the 1952 crop officially consisted of 8 billion puds and the true crop was 5½ billion. Quite a large exaggeration is involved. For about ten or fifteen years, the Soviets gave the real amount, but some years ago they adopted a different form of overestimate that means counting the grain in the combine harvester, with its earth and stones and water. This method is supposed to overestimate by only 20 percent.

MR. NOVAK: Would you, Dr. Dalrymple, tell us about the characteristics of Ukraine as a grain-producing area? I have always thought of Ukraine as the breadbasket of the world.

DR. DALRYMPLE: Famine was not new to the Soviet Union. Ukrainians and Russians had suffered in previous famines, particularly in the 1800s. Part of the problem is that much of the Soviet Union is not really very well suited to agriculture. In many areas farms operate on the margin in terms of growing season and rainfall. It does not take much to set agriculture back. The Ukraine, although it is the bread-basket of the country, is not immune to climate problems, but the soil itself is extremely fertile. I remember years ago seeing vast areas that had never been fertilized. Somebody from the West might have diffi-culty believing that productivity could be maintained without fertil-izer, but the soil was very good.

MR. NOVAK: Is that the black soil, the black earth we read about?

DR. DALRYMPLE: Yes. But more was involved in the case of the famine. The land was largely used for grain, and the Soviets were preoccupied with grain. The statistics for other crops indicate that the story was not quite as severe except in the case of livestock.

MR. NOVAK: Collectivization has always puzzled me. I had the impres-sion that because the growing season is relatively short, a large collec-tive effort had always been made at harvest time. True?

DR. DALRYMPLE: I am not so sure. If there was a joint effort, it was certainly a voluntary collective, which is quite different from a forced collective.

MR. NOVAK: No, I understood that it was voluntary but that resources had to be concentrated within a limited span of time.

DR. CONQUEST: Under the old system, which was the same as the medieval system in England, there was strip farming and the three-field system; every peasant had one, two, or three separate strips in one vast field and the same in the second and third fields. The strip in the third field had to lie fallow one year in three. The peasants had to coordinate the system of rotation. The village commune, which Marx misunderstood, served a productive purpose by facilitating coordina-tion and the selection of a field for cultivation the following year. The system was certainly cooperative, and although the Leninists and Gorki denounced the individualism of the peasant, the peasant had both individualism and cooperation, because cooperation implies in-dividualism. It is not the same as collectivism. It may have been a primitive way of operating, but it did show concern to protect the fertility of the land and to avoid overcropping. Lack of such concern in part accounts for the failure of the modern fertilizer-cum-tractor approach in the Soviet Union. People will not be bothered, and the man in charge of a province—like Larionov in Ryazan—will say, "I'll produce twice as much meat this year as they did last year." Then he slaughters everything in sight and imports meat and has to commit suicide, but the average official hopes for a transfer before the debacle so that his successor will take the blame. A bureaucrat cannot be a farmer.

DR. MACE: We should make one distinction, though. The Ukrainians did not cooperate with one another to the extent that the Russians did. The Ukrainians agriculturally had a much more individualistic tradition. Ukrainians did not have the village commune.

MR. NOVAK: Did this difference account for some of the antagonism between the Russians and the Ukrainians when people tried to identify kulaks?

DR. MACE: That is hard to say. "Kulak" is such a nebulous term. In some places anyone who had a piece of corrugated tin to keep the rain out would be a kulak, and the poorest person in the village might be called a *pidkurkulnyk, pobichnyk hlytaya,* roughly meaning kulak running dog, kulak henchman.

DR. CONQUEST: "Kulak" also refers to mentality, doesn't it?

DR. MACE: Yes, kulak mentality. It is really as much a political as a social phenomenon.

MR. NOVAK: And someone might be called a kulak even for psychological or spiritual reasons?

DR. MACE: Yes. A kulak was basically anyone the Soviets wanted to punish, for whatever reason.

MR. NOVAK: Do the deliberateness and the man-made nature of the famine seem explainable as a personal aberration or as a consequence of doctrine? The famine required an immense mobilization. To what extent would you attribute it to the character of Stalin and others like him and to what extent to a doctrine that is likely to express itself again in some fashion or another?

DR. CONQUEST: The famine cannot be regarded as the inevitable result of even a Stalin-type, collectivized, peasant economy. The Stalin-Kaganovich-Molotov leadership did have a decisive influence. We are somewhat in the position of asking whether a country would have gone to war if so-and-so had been prime minister. Perhaps it would not have; perhaps it would. Nevertheless, the Ukrainian peasantry did represent a special threat. Grigorenko takes the view, slightly different from ours, that the Stalin leadership felt hostility toward the Ukrainian peasantry because the Ukrainian peasantry had spoiled the first collectivization, the January-to-March crash collectivization. There certainly does seem to have been (at least this is my impression, and perhaps Jim Mace will correct me) much more resistance from the Ukrainian peasant, more rebellion, than appeared elsewhere. But the Ukrainian peasantry had been fighting the occupation for some time. The first Soviet governments operated only in the cities. Throughout the countryside were peasant rebellions, with peasant chiefs leading peasant armies of as many as up to 40,000. A very large number of the Ukrainian peasants had served in these armies; it might be fair to say that the majority supported the anti-Soviet armies. There was definitely what the British call bloody-mindedness among the Ukrainians against the regime.

MR. NOVAK: In other words, the motive was to punish as well as to subdue.

DR. CONQUEST: Yes, of course. The punishment of people who are troublemakers stems partly from a desire to subdue them as troublemakers.

DR. MACE: It was much harder for the Soviets to conquer Ukraine in the first place than to take control in Russia proper. The city of Kiev had twelve changes of government from 1917 to 1921. Not only did Denikin and the White Russian armies and the counterrevolutionaries and the Bolsheviks pass through, but there were also the Ukrainian nationalists, Petlyura, and the anarchist, Makhno. The Ukrainian revolution brought the largest area in history under anarchist sway.

The peasantry had an entirely different national tradition that was not based on a long history of serfdom. Serfdom came only at the time of Catherine the Great. The Russians had serfs far back in time, and certainly the system became universal, gaining legal sanction in 1649. Considerably more than 100 years passed before it reached the Ukrainian countryside. The basic national tradition in Ukraine centered on the Cossacks, who are very individualistic and fight back when things do not suit them. The structure of Soviet rule in the countryside in the 1920s indicates that the Soviets were more afraid of the Ukrainians than they were of the Russians. They retained the old Kombedy, the committees of the village poor, in the Ukrainian countryside until 1933, abolishing them in Russia in 1920. Ukraine was a sore spot, a place culturally, agriculturally, mentally, and spiritually very different from Russia and very self-assertive. The Soviets wanted to crush it.

Mr. Novak: What was the effect of the famine on the nationalities within the Soviet Union?

Dr. Mace: The famine—in fact, this period—is a watershed in Soviet nationalities policy. There is considerable difference between a history textbook from the 1920s and a textbook from the late 1930s, which is in many ways similar to textbooks being written today. In the 1920s, first, there was an apologetic attitude toward the different nationalities. The Soviets were sorry about Russian imperialism. They were saying, "All these peoples have achieved national liberation. We recognized that they have their own histories, that they do things their own way. We're all brothers, but they're different." Immediately after the famine, in 1934, there was a total turnabout in the way that the Soviet Union saw itself and in the way that Soviet history was taught. It was taught as Russocentric Soviet history, and something called Soviet patriotism, which is not very different from Russian nationalism, became the dominant ideology of the state. In the 1920s, the ideology held that the USSR was a more or less loose, heterogeneous confederation of nations banded together against imperialism, if you accept the rhetoric; after 1934 the Soviet Union was, even ideologically, basically Russia writ large. So the famine was crucial in the history of Soviet nationalities policy.

Mr. Novak: Could you describe the feelings of national identity that are present, if suppressed, in Ukraine today? Do we know enough about the matter to comment on it?

Dr. Mace: We have various sources of information. There is the Ukrainian dissident movement, including the Ukrainian Helsinki movement, which never disbanded. The Ukrainian Helsinki movement—it can be said—is alive and well and living in New Jersey. Most of its members are in the Gulag, but a few members are in the West now, and they formed an external group that represents the Ukrainian Helsinki movement. There was a period of official national self-assertion under the regime of Petro Shelest in the 1960s lasting until 1971. Shelest was purged, and there were massive arrests of Ukrainian intellectuals as part of what Ukrainians call the "general pogrom."

MR. NOVAK: The imprisonment of Moroz and others.

DR. MACE: Right, and there was imprisonment of a lot of people who are still there. Some of the statements coming from the Gulag are quite radical in the national sense, denouncing the Soviet government as a government of Russian occupiers of the Ukrainian nation. In one Ukrainian dissident publication in the early 1970s there was a call for the World Congress of Free Ukrainians to be recognized as the legitimate representative of the Ukrainian people until there could be a plebiscite. The Ukrainians do not like the Russian rule very much.

MR. NOVAK: In other words, there is still a very powerful political motive for continued silence about the famine?

DR. MACE: Oh, certainly.

MR. NOVAK: Before we turn to the cover-up, to its nature and its persistence, are there any more comments on the discussion thus far?

DR. CONQUEST: Compared with dissidence in Moscow, Ukrainian dissidence is remarkable in extent. It is found not only among literary intellectuals. Some of the people denounced are in the party's cultural apparatus.
Then there were two great riots in Ukraine. One had an economic cause, but the other involved nationalist slogans, as did the riots in Georgia. We have only very small pieces of evidence, but the potential for rebellion seems fairly high still, and this is certainly so in western Ukraine. In western Ukraine there are frequent complaints about people who have been sent to camps and who come back, that tens of thousands of them are still behaving badly. That complaint is very common. Western Ukraine still abounds with nationalists. Even the east has quite a few.

DR. MACE: The Soviets still occasionally uncover old cells of Ukrainian partisans, who are executed. These people are members of the organization of Ukrainian Nationalists, and the executions are announced in the Soviet press from time to time.

MR. NOVAK: Has there ever been, to shift now to the cover-up, a full-dress investigation of who said what in the Western press and why and what happened? Fifty years have now passed. Emotions should have cooled. What happened in the Western press?

DR. MACE: J. W. Crowl's *Angels in Stalin's Paradise*, a dissertation done at the University of Virginia that was published as an academic book not too long ago, is a study of Walter Duranty and Louis Fischer, two American journalists who were pivotal in suppressing the knowledge of the famine. The entire Western press corps knew about the famine. Malcolm Muggeridge said on many occasions and has written in his memoirs that *the* topic of conversation among the press corps was events in the South and the North Caucasus, and in Ukraine in particular. Duranty shocked his colleagues by telling them that things were even worse than they had heard, that millions of people were dying. Then Duranty, who was a *New York Times* correspondent and had just received a Pulitzer Prize for his own generally sympathetic reportage of Soviet life, proceeded to publish articles skeptical of the "famine scare," in which he asserted that there was some hunger but no starvation in south Russia. Most of the Western correspondents, particularly in the English-speaking world, did not report what was going on even though they knew about it.

DR. CONQUEST: There was quite a lot of reporting. The Hearst press had sources—very good sources, not just correspondents. Some of these sources were American Communists who had been there, like Tawdul, who gave very clear firsthand accounts. These were people who had been around for months. Chamberlin, for example, reported very accurately. Even the pro-Soviet people such as Hindus give us an account that is not altogether sympathetic, nearer truth than falsehood, at least. Duranty was described in his citation for the Pulitzer Prize as "unprejudiced," but in fact he misreported. Still, Muggeridge was writing for the *Manchester Guardian*. The *Daily Telegraph* certainly had reports, the *Times* had reports, and there were also reports in *Figaro*. Many of the great papers in the West printed reports. The answer to your question "Was the story suppressed in the Western press, was it unavailable?" is no. Still, as Susan Sontag points out, if the Hearst press is automatically dismissed from consideration, then the story was not available to Americans.

DR. DALRYMPLE: The press seems not to have pursued the story with the same ferocity that it would show today. The accounts seem to have been more isolated and did not add up.

DR. CONQUEST: At a certain point, reporters were not allowed back in Ukraine. I forget the date.

DR. MACE: That was a danger too, of course. The reporters had very little chance to travel in Ukraine, and if they violated the rules they were given no further chances, so there was really very little chance for on-site investigation that was not rigged ahead of time.

MR. NOVAK: It's true too, isn't it, that if you intended to stay as a reporter in Moscow . . . ?

DR. MACE: You did not report the famine.

MR. NOVAK: Your visa could be revoked because of unfavorable reporting. It appears that the general facts of the matter were reported accurately enough, but the reports did not change public perceptions.

DR. MACE: No, that is true. Still, we must first understand how people saw the Soviet Union during this period. These were the years of the Great Depression, and stories about human suffering were not considered big news. You or I could go out on any street corner and see people suffering. To the extent that people took a great interest in the Soviet Union, they did so thinking that maybe this was an alternative for the West, that maybe the Soviets were trying to build a future that would work. There was a certain pro-Soviet bias in many of the English-language newspapers. Generally, the farther east in Europe, the better the reporting. The English and Americans did not have much material on the famine, although it was possible for readers to find out what was going on. There was more in Germany, Switzerland, and Austria. The Polish press had significant coverage, and of course the best was the western Ukrainian press. Very detailed and very graphic accounts appeared in *Dilo*, which was the main Ukrainian-language newspaper in Polish-ruled western Ukraine.

MR. NOVAK: Again, the reason was that western Ukraine at this point was in Poland.

DR. MACE: Right. The newspaper was heavily censored, but it was censored in the Polish style, which was more authoritarian than totalitarian. Blank spaces indicated deletions. The copy was not censored from the very outset, however. Much could also be learned from the Ukrainian language press in the West, in this country and in Canada.

MR. NOVAK: How do you react to the Soviets' repeated assertion, which I heard often enough in my short stay at the United Nations, that they lost 20 million people in the war and that this loss establishes the Soviet Union's commitment to peace?

DR. MACE: It is tragic that the Soviets lost 20 million people in the Second World War, but when we compare that figure to the number of people who died in the 1930s, it seems not quite as immense. The two numbers are not so very different in order of magnitude, and we are comparing wartime losses with peacetime.

DR. CONQUEST: There is rather more to the matter, according to Maksudov. I reached the same figure that he did, but by a different method. The actual number killed by the Germans was probably about 15 million. The war casualties are given by Stalin as 7 million—I mean the soldier casualties. The same number of civilian casualties is about the most we can assume. The Soviets invented the figure of 20 million; it has never been documented, even in speeches. It does not matter particularly. Maksudov, however, takes the view that another 15 million died in the Soviet Union in the same period through Soviet action. Certainly, between, say, 1937 and 1953, there cannot have been fewer than 1 million a year dying in the labor camps. So these figures, as Jim Mace says, are comparable to those for deaths in peacetime or from Soviet action. Whether the figure for war losses is 7 million or 15 million, it far exceeds the number of Western casualties; the British casualties were about half a million. But oddly enough, the ruling bodies show a completely different incidence of death. Only one member of the Central Committee was killed, but the number on the memorial in the House of Commons is twenty-nine. (One Central Committee member went over to the Germans—but we exclude him.) Given that the leaders were spared, why should the Central Committee mind war?

DR. MACE: Stalin once told Churchill that the war itself was in no sense as big, as difficult, for him personally as collectivization had been.

MR. NOVAK: Before we conclude, are there any other matters that we should address?

DR. DALRYMPLE: Dr. Conquest commented earlier that the accounts of the individual survivors show a remarkable degree of consistency. The same is true on a larger scale with respect to other accounts of the famine. Much of the reading matter is rather terrifying, yet it all seems to fit one broad pattern. I have read very little that does not somehow fit. This consistency is remarkable. Most major public events inspire very different opinions or points of view on the course of events.

DR. CONQUEST: You made a point about proof. In this sort of history we do not have proof. We will not have the memoirs of Kaganovich, but this is the normal state of affairs in history except for the very recent history of a few countries in the West. In writing about practically any historical event almost anywhere in the world, we necessarily proceed on the evidence of odd particulars. The evidence is not complete, and some people reject conclusions, saying that they cannot be proved—they say, for example, that we cannot prove Hitler ordered the Holocaust. David Irving says so. No, it cannot be proved in the sense that we have unfortunately come to expect in certain other sorts of scholarship; we do not necessarily have documentary proof. Yet we do not have to have proof in the same sense; historical proof is different. Gibbon discussed this matter extremely well in his *Vindication*. The incontrovertibility of the evidence can be plain even when it is not documentary or complete.

MR. NOVAK: We have been talking about one of the saddest events of recent history, one that occurred during the lifetime of many of the people present in this room. It seems appropriate to end with the thought that a most important function of the human spirit is to remember, both to recall and to learn. The exercise of remembering is part of our obligation to our fellows everywhere. The work of historians therefore plays a crucial function in the life of the human spirit.

Further Reading

Ammende, Ewald. *Human Life in Russia*. London: Allen & Unwin, 1936.

Antonov-Ovseyenko, Anton. *The Time of Stalin*. New York: Harper & Row, 1981.

Black Deeds of the Kremlin: A White Book, Vol. II, The Great Famine in Ukraine in 1932–33. Detroit: Dobrus, 1955.

Carynnyk, Marco. "The Famine the 'Times' Couldn't Find," *Commentary*, November 1983.

———. "The New York Times and the Great Famine," *The Ukrainian Weekly*, September 11 and 18, 1983.

Chamberlin, William Henry. *Russia's Iron Age*. Boston: Little, Brown and Co., 1934.

———. *The Ukraine: A Submerged Nation*. New York: Macmillan, 1944.

Conquest, Robert. *The Great Terror: Stalin's Purges of the Thirties*. New York: Macmillan, 1968.

Crowl, James William. *Angels in Stalin's Paradise: Western Reporters in Soviet Russia, 1917 to 1937, A Case Study of Louis Fischer and Walter Duranty*. Washington, D.C.: University Press of America, 1982.

Dalrymple, Dana. "The Soviet Famine of 1932–1934," *Soviet Studies*, no. 3 (1964) and no. 3 (1965).

Dushnyck, Walter. *50 Years Ago: The Famine Holocaust in Ukraine*. New York: World Congress of Free Ukrainians, 1983.

The Great Famine in Ukraine: The Unknown Holocaust. Jersey City, N.J.: Ukrainian Weekly, 1983.

Haliy, Mykola. *The Organized Famine in Ukraine, 1932–33*. Chicago: Ukrainian Research and Information Institute, 1963.

Hryshko, Wasyl. *The Ukrainian Holocaust of 1933*. Toronto: Bahriany Foundation, 1983.

Karatnycky, Adrian. "Famine That the West Forgot," *Wall Street Journal*, July 7, 1983.

Koestler, Arthur. *The Yogi and the Commissar and Other Essays*. New York: Macmillan, 1967.

Kopelev, Lev. *The Education of a True Believer*. New York: Harper & Row, 1980.

Kostiuk, Hryhory. *Stalinist Rule in the Ukraine: A Study of the Decade of Mass Terror (1929–39)*. New York: Praeger, 1961.

Kravchenko, Victor. *I Chose Freedom: The Personal and Political Life of a Soviet Official*. New York: Charles Scribner's Sons, 1946.

Kuropas, Myron B. "America's 'Red Decade' and the Great Famine Cover-up," *The Ukrainian Weekly*, March 20, 1983.

Lyons, Eugene. *Assignment in Utopia*. 1937. Reprint. Westport, Conn.: Greenwood Press, 1971.

Mace, James E. *Communism and the Dilemmas of National Liberation: National Communism in Soviet Ukraine, 1918–1933.* Cambridge, Mass.: Harvard University Press, 1983.

————. "The Man-Made Famine of 1933 in Soviet Ukraine: What Happened and Why," *Almanac of the Ukrainian National Association.* Jersey City, N.J., 1983.

Muggeridge, Malcolm. *Chronicles of Wasted Time: Volume One: The Green Stick.* New York: Morrow, 1973.

————. *Winter in Moscow.* Boston: Little, Brown and Co., 1934.

Pidhainy, S.O., ed. *The Black Deeds of the Kremlin: A White Book.* Vols. 1, 2. Toronto-Detroit: Dobrus, 1953, 1955.

Sullivant, Robert S. *Soviet Politics and the Ukraine, 1917–1957.* New York: Columbia University Press, 1962.

U.S. Congress, House of Representatives, Committee on the Judiciary. *Testimony of Dr. Lev Dobriansky,* September 23, 1964.

Woropay, Olexa. *The Ninth Circle: In Commemoration of the Victims of the Famine of 1933.* Cambridge, Mass.: Ukrainian Studies Fund, 1983.